Syncopations

Also by Laressa Dickey

Bottomland
Roam
Twang

Laressa Dickey

Syncopations

Shearsman Books

First published in the United Kingdom in 2019 by
Shearsman Books
50 Westons Hill Drive
Emersons Green
BRISTOL
BS16 7DF

Shearsman Books Ltd Registered Office
30–31 St. James Place, Mangotsfield, Bristol BS16 9JB
(this address not for correspondence)

www.shearsman.com

ISBN 978-1-84861-659-2

Contents

American Sonnet

Come sit beside my sad story of six hearted cowboys
who throw dirt into holes they have dug for their brothers
whose bodies walked around topped by bearskin caps
who stacked suitcases, siphoned gas from Exxon
who spoke twice from the mouth with pits for hands
who spit courtesy of Red Man, *ask him if he don't*
whose mothers as girls dug holes in the ground to dump failed bakings
who know when there are cows upstream
where Davy Crocket dreams only of his own teeth
which are stained and pocked by the great weed
which grew in hotbeds and cured inside other people's barns—
who called it *tabbaq* from those Arabs you can't stand as early as the 9th
 century, & lo
for matches one must mince many firs to make Diamonds
for head and tinder shall not impede the spark

A Word In Edgewise

Here: you are
Now that's better

I wanted the birthing, when it didn't make no nevermind

Jealous retroactive spoon in four forked cups
Fill the spoon with gladness

Context: grain in wood, and you
swallow anyway, talk with mouth full

But is this about you   fields soaked; money slim – then how not to feel sorry

You walk with too-flat feet

A too-flat sound

It's personal   Calm down

What can I say about your experience? The pearl
and its great price sliding under the bed

next to me. Looking under water for change: matches

Fair start, corpse in corn

Elm. Oleander. Crack in the sidewalk, tubers

My point is fluidity

Flow; no jabs unless it's necessary
Plan on sleeping

I am what you have   big change
toward train-track sparks

What's the time? Should we be here now

Ask, what makes your heart race

Squall full of black birds silhouetted: trees backlit in a spray of flight

It's right there   I never said that

As if I would care

The mark of a woman
making of a table

The last time I was a character
I keep saying: keep saying

When there is no place to speak, what is there

When the field floods, which way to the bargains

Tuning

The father's life wound around a grandfather clock and ticked.

On a church pew or a behind a one-seater truck cab
or riding on the back of flatbed over new asphalt.

Occasional bugs in the face.

A cemetery for every town, fresh flowers on military holidays.

oo

Often that bad taste was dirt, lettuce from ground after all, so strawberry, so turnip greens. Poke salad wild next to woodpiles, especially after a field was cleared. I hated vinegar of greens but cleaned plates.

oo

Mary a holy name, albeit simple.

A word like *bastard* driven by foot sole into dirt.

I bet that Aristotle person got the shit kicked out of him.
Certainly if he were a woman running off at the mouth.

oo

If this land was once covered by sea, they won't teach that sort of past here. Pass the tobacco stalk down the line. There's rhythm they say I don't have, and they work with it like ghosts. So what. I feel someone talking to me.

oo

wandered as fat
pigeon even I
loathing

oo

My brother, big bodied, sobbing. We were sweet and vulnerable. Our father raised Caucasian bees, which were seductive. Women flew through our skies in blue skirts. Early I took a creek path only to see red clover blooming. What could happen that they would not see? The roses belonged for years, small napes sending them downstream. He took off his glasses, watched the old barn burn to ash. Even though I could only smell pig and salt, once I smelled cat's milk. All these stones, fresh mint on the banks.

Tonight I'll play fiddle and may break the strings.
What other place is sensed with dancing?

oo

My mistake, filling the curve of letters into square little boxes.

oo

My grandmother's body did its best to kill off girl children.

Do I know the ancestry of my teaching?

One got through.
One girl came through –

∞

Imagine how your breasts appear once and then wither, same day. This before you climb the hill with your mother. And by hill I mean the one between you and the neighbor. By creek, by country road. To look across night to bonfire, bright in his hayfield. But too there's mean men, all men being mean, tracing circles around the fire. A ceremony around a Jesus-less cross bobbing in the fire. 1989.

∞

Before daughter I was swept up in mimosa; he smiled

Ran races barefoot. Beat boys, girls.

Before breasts, before gabs and nodes of worthlessness, just green hills and patterns of thought going around the jaw line and closing it.

Before a man says *you just need better shoes*, the ordinary magic of a girl sleeping peacefully in her own bed. I shift the sheets around for her.

I saw him struggle putting his bag down

Just one crow and me, we saw him trip

∞

Mary a *holy* name.

oo

A woman running off at the mouth and he couldn't take it. With no regard for the order numbers came in, being tied to a wall at various angles.

oo

Your own woman.

The illusion of simultaneity.

oo

This evening in which I love. In which older mysteries, in both hands.
Off the clothesline.
                    A buttered evening in which I wear
all the luminous voices. I was a man
I shrieked.

All the trees I had to level to do this.

oo

What makes it special how one writes letters in dark to a backward self, your little keeper, running under windows with willow.

oo

wore chambers –
porches
for hours

oo

Or dream of filling out breasts where before only ribs
crossing repeat to cage to heart, horizon

even now phrases as drudgery.
Grease from a week's dishes on the bottom of the sink.

Tourniquets, let me squeeze all the privates
out of this version. A door

pincher bug telling the future—

oo

Suffering, as you say, from natural defectiveness.

oo

A chain link dog pen around this, a peacock in the pen, named Joe.

A tree grows inside a boy and later when fruit comes he must pucker, as if eating persimmons.

oo

Dandy she thinks. In this infernal pressing of grey down on her person, a map of her places, see here too where her room stands on the second floor. A boy crying upstairs.

oo

Where did my body learn to rush?

There.

Someone waiting for an object. Hatchet, wrench, ratchet, chainsaw, circle saw, jigsaw, turpentine, paintbrush, shovel, rake, hoe, post hole digger, bailing twine, electric fence, barbed wire, screwdriver, hammer, drill bits, level, plunger, duct tape, caulk, pliers, vise grip, spackle, hacksaw, screws, nails, electrical tape, anchor, pry bar, square, caliper, drill, scratch awl, sledgehammer, stud finder, tin snips, tobacco stakes

If not public, I don't exist—

oo

Sparrows about our feet someone there tossed seeds

oo

This the way I don't feel it.

oo

From the hilltop all men, a circle of 30, distinguished sets of costumes and by circle I mean circle around a fire in a field where that fire ate a cross and by that I mean there were others too, not only white ghost uniforms but some in drabs and shaved heads, *New Nazis* they said and to the hayfield on a road on which hardly anyone drove they had come. They sang a little song called White Power. All drunk, half dancing, half limping, trying not to fall, in a circle around a fire destined to eat that Jesus-less cross.

On top of a hill, an *I*, lying very still and watching. I wore my old jeans and a Mickey Mouse sweatshirt.

oo

A musk bend
slip slop
ascension

oo

They didn't want anyone to know
They wanted to announce
They kept their money in cash pressed straight in the Bible
They turned away from windows
They opened curtains
reported daily happenings: 4 bantam eggs, dead mouse

oo

Church bells. I was waiting for someone in this house to get up.

oo

Years later Mr. D told, when asked about that night, how his grandson sat in the dark on his own porch, shotgun across his lap, alone. How he sat listening to the chanting when suddenly (like a lark I mean to say he was 10) a voice on the loudspeaker:

DOES ANYONE HAVE A FIRE EXTINGUISHER?

oo

She the tiny snake-killing mother. Held over her head so all rattles would be included in the photograph and not bleed into grass. Her second weapon a hoe the head came right off. This is how you live in woods with small children. That man with a red beard loved The Statler Brothers. Ears red, his people from grudge bearers, standing in line.

oo

A tiny grave grows inside a boy.

oo

The map a space where inner and outer body is one thing,
like thick syrup, honey

just breath and break of space to speak

I rely on you to help me hold this, a place for speech

a place for us to meet,

return—

◦◦

Dried chins.
Dried corn.
She wolf.

◦◦

The titles of things they call dreams, other people's offices.
The dead, the day.
Every time I look away fish jump.

◦◦

My people love and sing to me. A woman her wooden heart. So my lungs so run repeat. Born of atom, that world lament. Together worn, fruit-bearing, in halves.

◦◦

He gave his father-in-law permission to dump old appliances in a ditch on the backside of his own land. Color televisions, refrigerators, PVC pipe, can openers, stove, microwave, washers and dryers, a piece of old plow. Years went by and the pile stacked up. When floods came, and ditches all over the county emptied, all these lifted up and dumped out in the field where his own father, wearing a straw fedora, had often broken ground standing on a plow pulled by two faithful mules.

∘∘

Wings and legs, everyone wanted to talk to her. Tired and woke tired. Bicycles, circadian objects. Someone being watched as the hips were squared. All night people become carcasses. Do you want to stay here she asks. I'm working up to something.

∘∘

Don't mind Novocain, I saw how adults took pills. What was inside came out. As in, my body is mad. Why spokes inside my skull.

Pressure cooker on the stove. And the way everybody works so we can pay the farm payment, which we owe to the bank, which owns us. When work is not dictated by others, then it is dictated down the line.

∘∘

I slipped in water
She could smell smoke on her books
Morning broke
As when things move back to a center
I didn't care about form anymore
The house was sparkly
My combs shone
Anything like cat piss was overwhelming
Distal breakers
Even my wrist came from another generation

Natural they say you keep accumulating years
Potted plants, just his tree with a whole forest hanging on it
A face or just a chin on the surface of the waters

oo

Hang on a minute. I gotta yell at 2 dogs.

oo

Seed potatoes
Somehow *thank you* didn't seem to say enough
To share a town with those who plotted
A broken bat
There the nervous system takes over
Does she wish she was someone
Small boys passing with fathers holding hands
I am lost and the people here are lost
You might be able to keep the drain clear
If beauty can make anything

oo

I'm fixing to paint you a picture of this.

You was sitting
on the steps.
                                        I done told you.

It's just the one lady that lives in town.
                                                I been living here too.

I done what you told me.

Knowed you was a fool.

∘∘

He was ahead of me walking

I was six   I wasn't a witch

Behold the capital—
underbelly of plants stuck in the ground

To look around   through fence   through bottleneck

Except workdays when he drove the mule or spit tobacco juice;
stood on the plow and didn't need your goddamned atlas

I carried rust in my hands and spread it out over the window

Everything was temporary

We watched and didn't speak

There is no death   this is why I can't look directly

Half Rest

We had our life together and then suddenly didn't. There was blue sky but the previous night was bright in the hollow, the gold distant out my window. I slept in a pink room, under pink covers.

oo

Just the week before, the cutting as in   we gotta cut the pigs. Castrate them I mean, the smell of ________ and high pitched squealing. Here again, begging off.

oo

There was no place to go, at night. Walks stirring up faces, bob WHITE!

oo

Night a function of looking and seeing. All buttresses descend. What was there, just shapes: Y, ash, milk bowl.

I can't help wondering what they did with all the testicles, at least 40 feeder pigs x 2, that's 80, friends.

oo

Whether we called the rescue squad and they didn't come, or whether it was too late when Ronnie Parker knocked. The only sow we named broke out.

The feeder pigs broke out.

Pigs can panic

others in space suits

rather confident
smile

Love a companion to violence

oo

There are myths
and many working to erase them

I prefer moths
on each of my finger
tips

I have never been to Alaska
but imagine it cunning

My back is my tenderloin

Wandering vine turns green I
can't stand it

Wasn't it grey yesterday, wasn't it just yesterday
o for the drizzle, moths

oo

can only tell you what broke out, was it only yesterday, was it then milk
ran out, moths ate through the thin wool, wasn't it yesterday,

orange in the tangerine the only bright thing

the only bright thing

Cleavers

We had already been in the house together before we made it

There had been birthday mail, something woven into the rug of Nomads, our hair falling absently into it, flowering among the weft

Nothing should complicate this

The dead tree slowly came full with buds, the shoots sick with starlight, hovering

It was here we arranged the stones; the sight of all this was the memory of its taste on my tongue from years before

You gave me credit

We began to say things and also to feel complexly about spare rooms. I felt certain I had bathed you in everything secret

They said we could only do one thing at a time

I recognized myself in the water, where my grip on daily practices creates interesting trouble

As when Ms. Hay said *if you don't do the Bedoin solo I'll kill myself*

About his stale smoke, all those chairs, the wooden puffs in mushroom in the first place

I began dreaming in houses, lured to sleep looking for hardwood tongue and grooves to match

Now also the smoke on your coat

Free you with the things we'll put down; all the wadded paper in your hands those little birds from morning awake

Too late too late and the *cha cha cha* in the background

Ficus second to the rubber trees bring your father back to life

Something behind me 10 paces spreading middle of my back,

Bread crumbs

Two Holed Mouth

Note differences between the Nashville Warbler and the Tennessee Warbler.

"The Nashville's song is of rather greater volume, beginning with a longer, more deliberate prelude of four or five notes, and ending in a short, rapidly weakening trill or slide; while the song of the Tennessee has a brief prelude, with a long finishing trill increasing in loudness and intensity to an abrupt ending… Both songs are unmusical."

—*Bird Portraits in Color*, Thomas Sadler Roberts

Mandolin Man

the dance floor   is empty

won't your

HONKYTONK Band

play the last song for me?

Take me   awayyyyyyyyyyyyyyy

my soul's feelin' empty.

My heart's
in your hands

Mandolin Man

Everyone hid things in small chests

No one body moved much   place to place

We knew how to look
The only thing tuned   the piano   the radio

No one listening

And with no reference points   a train line
Nashville to California

one might think of swapping farms
might think of picking guitar

Except cycles and well-worn

Ms Icie on her front porch   a green metal chair
fat hands around a glass of sweet tea

Nearby the mechanic –

Nearby this movement as it happens

Miles and miles between Nashville, California
by train;   so many charmed

Neal S. rode it all the way, maybe to swap the farm
for one in California   *My God*, he said

After going, standing over
flying dust   tumbleweeds

the heel of his boot   that small twist around
toward home   *My God*, he said

I wouldn't take all the land in California
for Ms Sally Hannah's feedlot.

That's the lot full of cowshit   sparrows

castoff grain

oo

It was a secret how. No one seen afterwards. Breastbones turned inward, in certain flowers, a slight whistle. A keel, a keening. Natal down, a first fall plumage, some considered it commendable to kill them. Various others capture the thumping love song, one that sounds like a man driving a stake in the ground some place far in the distance.

oo

Some believed tissues of the inner ear formed
a child's beginning
before other senses
so the ear tunes very early
to the twang of its surroundings

oo

I was a moon-walker. The first to walk in another world. To the very edge of atmosphere, my free-body diagrams under my arms. First words, kick, jump. I had hallelujah even though the days died. The voice a tool that magnified everything; that wildness lying on top of my body breathed when I did.

oo

Orbit, until this. Now the talking inside. When small they just shook you till you resonated, now a kick in the organs. I a witness coming, going. We changed roles; he did not want to become nothing again.

°°

A small bright cross emerges
in night sky's dark
centered in a picture window

The laws of speech not mine

Wooden house, golden
child eyes, child speech
only questions

Why do those ghosts burn Jesus?

°°

Some glad morning
we weren't creating history on that level

a rust-proof corset
no breast or healing

only semaphore
do you see me

Just a few more days
guaranteed in simple terms

The surfacing human works if we agree

A woman twirling, a kiss

fragile, this game

heart steady   This articulate decorum

I needed a way to disappear/consensus bears down

You test the limit/withdraw politely

I became my own lab animal/people shuffle

Once you could vote, well that wasn't a real voice

What is the illusion we are sitting together on?

How could I survive talking?

/slow/but no one waits/to negotiate

To say there is nothing here in this decorum,

a head tilting to look at your face

Tuning makes it cinematic

Tuning is   a kind of sitting

How do you know where you are in a room

when the room is gone

We are always testing precision and defining territory,

a kiss, tools

                                                            to interrupt

°°

His chest a barrel for words they come
no time to speak she so busy

I must plant my seeds today
or be lost to them

How much accomplished I would not say at breakfast

California valley filled with hatching dragonflies
                                        into my windshield

                        Swarms with no sound
I remember a thunderstorm coming

Light cut by black oaks dimly on hills

I was less sure then

At night soaked ourselves in the obvious fact we had no culture

Say goodbye to the Banyan for me

already coming up in words, sprouting

°°

You must hold space for your own I; otherwise someone fills it

Never took to roses, flabby arms, petals dropping off I passed

Enough feeling separate: your legs, your legs   Who loves like she loves?

Born there a circle of mountains around you

Stuck in your country with little way to know poplars
Assumed I loved what you loved

The ladder at cross-purposes   slung on your arm

                                        The street smells like our pig barn
Assumed I can't be seen rehearsing chase scenes

oo

How a body's trace made in spaces   particular

I lost the kite of Winter you talk your way through

What about footprints on the roof? I ask but the ghost of what I know appears

Dog and bird, carcass in teeth; later the underscore
of hammer dulcimer

oo

No one in woods shouts

If he steps over the timing   fence pushing weight to work

They hated traitors, cowards especially

All the electricity coming through   that hospitality

I never realized I had an accent until –
Maria from the Dakotas chain smoked Lucky Strikes

The problem with her books I wasn't sure how the words should sound

Can't count on people leaving you alone here

Their talk a repeat   Did I have anything my own?

Someone else's thick mouth swallowing songs

oo

Oak. We asleep to cricket legs. Johnson Grass. When someone started a sentence, we knew the next. Little fortune-tellers. Both sides with predictable and unforgivable qualities but only seeing the other. Sweetgum Tree. Near the end of her life Estelle preferred her false teeth in a waterglass, having perfected slicing the hot dog so it splayed over two slices of white bread. Government cheese, two months in her freezer. She wanted help digging holes in her yard, but we too busy driving place to place. Kudzu. This town its big spring. Beech Nut.

What was barbaric? People unrecognizable by their speech.

oo

a masculinity so dominant so perverse

relegates its objects to hiding, to be transparent its _______
for violence much as it ever was

I stopped singing, afraid God took my voice

People said things like *I'm going to stomp you* –
A feeling in trees, as if they remembered and therefore the potential

oo

Lily-livered
holed in hills

They call it brotherhood
but wore robes to hide themselves even from

Length of phrase
When to end and begin again

A character who cannot leave
is one who will not stop moving

°°

The rhythm of vowels changed. The speed faster when I called home from California; my mother and not a word what I said

°°

original condition
stranger

Many times overstayed
I had not seen the end

°°

One reciting sounds over a lifetime, which bothers no one.

Where is the voice?

Under rocks?

Every bit of speech a conversion.

oo

a song sparrow

spine

spine

spine

spine

pine

oo

quality of voice,

he talked the hind legs off a mule; till he was blue in face; tall tales; spun a web; chewed fat;

echo

echo

echo

echo

spun

here –

here?

here.

sound from the back of the throat;

a girl
with no door
on her mouth
(Sophocles)

oo

echo how to explain twang of others *echo* how to account that it was possible to alter *echo* all that is raw and formless *echo* that undomesticated *echo* biting tongue rather than say something gets her in *echo* does your voice have too much in *echo* shouting unacceptable *echo* contortion I make to talk to you *echo* this something we decided together *echo* sorry for them, if indeed it was their sentiment *echo* saying, what you want *echo* with tenderness *echo* what's it to you *echo* writing a book? *echo* her stepsister and stepmother complained about her behind, how mean, how like a man *echo* a woman would be agreeable, easy to manage, industrious and even cheerful *echo* something saying inside of saying *echo* couldn't ask them to the funeral or do over *echo* lost *echo* lost *echo* lost everyone lost *echo* my learning a time a bomb *echo* men straight *echo* ladies curving *echo* men good *echo* ladies evil *echo* can't sit still *echo* opposites in fog *echo* for prudence and moderation *echo* goober *echo* voodoo *echo* all my double modals *echo* I might could do that for you *echo* used to could dance a jig *echo* this here *echo* this here *echo* I'm fixing to quit *echo echo* a-hootin' a-hollerin' *echo* what we fail to understand *echo* is death theater enough *echo* if brokenness isn't end *echo* empire implodes *echo* as stripping tobacco eats the bodies *echo* life always a corpse standing straight as if life at stake *echo* a girl waits for someone to water *echo* one can learn how to be delicate *echo* simply standing holding a flower in your hand 7 years *echo* when you are old you will have become famous *echo* no one here has lost teeth *echo* generation to generation *echo* you don't see the moon *echo* just the space I am pointing to

Whole Rest

The father does not dry dishes or buy soap.
The father does not fly in an airplane.
The father does not wear a woolen overcoat.
The father does not leave.
The father does not pinch new leaves off basil.
The father does not give account of himself.
The father does not write down recipes.
The father does not trouble himself with moths.
The father does not collect moss between stones along canals.
The father does not believe in wool.
The father does not throw out his just-swept dust.
The father does not cut cheese into tiny cubes.
The father does not collect Weck jars or quilt Rooster pillow tops.
The father does not vacillate, fry bacon, pace.
The father does not look at maps.
The father does not ride a bicycle.
The father does not negotiate walking with a thousand people down a
    shopping street.
The father does not fit himself in small stairs.
The father does not put holes in the walls for blue to come through.
The father does not run out to meet his lover.
The father does not walk down a canal hoping to find a second hand shop
    for the good of the people and low prices for Persian hallway rugs
    with handwritten labels in ink on the back so as to identify the
    precise city where the rug was made.

The father does not swim or float in the sea.
The father does not boulder.
The father does not stand in the rain with his head tilted and mouth
    open to the sky.
The father does not move a terrapin out of the road.
The father does not cross town by foot to buy cheese.
The father does not weave, write with chalk.

The father does not lie, does not have use for tropical plants.
The father does not swoon.
The father does not cry at beauty.
The father does not use small spoons.
The father does not bleed, wonder about the orange farmer's worn hands
or where he got his pocketknife.
The father does not eat in hospitals, or learn to count time.
The father does not stop and fold his legs.
The father does not debone.
The father does not think in doses.
The father does not walk into rooms backwards or carry his weight
inflated in his lungs.

The father does not pull out long grey hairs.
The father does not dream of being a pilot.
The father does not clap or have arthritic feet.
The father does not wait.
The father does not use public transportation or live without woodpeckers.
The father does not regulate the cycles of others.
The father does not lie in bed waiting for the dream to finish.
The father does not shuffle.
The father does not sort.
The father does not hallelujah or trip on the hem of his pants.
The father does not stand for 10 minutes sensing his spine.

The father does not split.
The father does not practice writing his own name.
The father does not question conversions.
The father does not shovel snow or think of snow globes when looking
out windows at snow.

The father does not collect rocks, seeds of chestnut trees in foreign countries.
The father does not smell of lavender.
The father does not make editions, installations, knit tiny folding hearts.
The father does not want the rugs to stop sliding around.
The father does not train the ficus.
The father does not write from right to left in a curving, feminine script.

The father does not doodle.
The father does not go out for stamps.

Pitch

You must take care of your own endings

so you don't lessen them   or keep going –

We practice all the endings, for example

You will have to train your arms to reach again

Tuning

The letter a chart, shows conversions, altitudes.

The mean sea level begins in Amsterdam, where Europe begins, with the Zuider Zee. Which is what my grandmother said, in a poem she wrote about her grandfather's migration from Belgium, via Holland, to the US. Belgium, Holland, it was all the same to us, this beautiful stone of a story lost in tobacco rows, in the welder's arc, buried behind the shop out back of the house.

oo

So you believe in God? I was raised Catholic but recently became a Methodist. Such joyful people. I mean, people either believe in God or they don't. So do you? My son doesn't. At least, I don't think so.

oo

How did your mother feel about being female?

How does a woman from Tennessee take her shirt off?

They taught me how to shoot a gun.
I learned to open the traps and set starlings free.

What does she believe about her body?

Drove them crazy with the questions

Of her opals

oo

My letter writing gotten behind really sorry. Summer, a big way, climbing temperatures, 94 degrees. The men mowing their clothes wet with sweat, we take then what they send. Stay in when the temp is less than 25 and over 85 I say, seems like a dream the right to worry, your mother spoke about Master leading you.

B. isn't strong enough to come. No one recovers as fast. A touch of vertigo, but bright dozens, a lot of singing but no names. Boys behaving like big men like weeds

you have time, be your sweet self

oo

In Tuscany on her first visit overseas my mother walked through Italian pastures in the heat of the day, looking for what?

I wanted to say my spine full of holes, in what city was that possible –

I failed to mention

A simpler existence would be to play cards

Many things I didn't know how to talk about

like when she poured boiling water in the sink
without telling me

Why couldn't she just wear lavender and be silent,
now I have to be quiet for both of us

oo

Without her dentures my grandmother grew tired

I pled, I was in a hurry, our feet in to cool

He began to chauffeur, carrying kids to Nashville
we couldn't get nothing; plenty of food but no money to buy it

First the show barn—cows exercised daily to keep men from starving

What did you do, girl, when you went to fetch the water?

oo

I never met them. Never shopped, never handled the money.

Some things was give to us, thrilled, say, to get oats.

Kids throwing shoes out a car window on the drive home

I picked enough cotton to buy some wine serge
make a skirt

Even rich folks didn't have rugs on the floors;
for us depression started

I ought to wear you out girl!

When we could, we'd buy 100 pounds of sugar.

Turn around in the row, I mean, I flew

oo

She believed her body was small, and she inside it.
Been told she was a girl, two others died before.

Should she have lived? She lived.

A pony to make her taller.
Thank goodness a mother who hemmed and sewed.

oo

Switch sick ones, places with the dead
Someone already parking there

[Elders can decide, from looking, whether the child understands]

I am a firm nest below the nets

oo

A little note stopped me, you on my mind
placing autumn inching I do little jobs get ready

Your mother looks years younger she had her hair cut
Cold days hard and steady thinking you every day

So nice you're trying out how the Eskimos lived
maybe if I was your age

if I say matter, matter in my mouth in hand
swallowed whole?

What stayed an outside world   this molded me
I separate the placings

No that didn't happen, my pardons, in between they laugh

hate very hot days   buttercups dark windy
peeping up jasmine wind

I'm lonely for my neighbor she's good to me   her neck
arteries blocked   concern [concern nodding]

When I was young, thought I'd be a missionary to Belgian Congo
that work thrilled me

Other things in the way
maybe not for me to follow I wonder?

Your envelope fascinated me I tried to repeat

little schism they say she'll be a long time

my dirty house   part of the morning I spoke with her

She was ill sunny days

she may come home little mother I'm sure

∘∘

not a trace or model,
but an actual map

Places one could get back to
as in where the boundary between countries is crossed

I searched but couldn't remember roads that led to our old place

Here I do not hide

As I with my long arms and three steps for Winter allow

For the cotton has become
Or the wool will begin: you bring along

oo

resist talking about his life and body because this I always eclipsed

oo

I have a sense / the body / again again
what to do / upon accident / disqualification / is, is personal
to lose face / I say / this is how I work /

there are moments I cannot find my way back to / muscles

balancing then / becomes the task

this is how to make a map of the body inside
that house of you

oo

Tried the gesture, fell over from a heavy head. To surprise myself again. A light duet, are there ways besides repeating everything. From these little exorcisms from these little losses, watch don't speak, or speak don't watch, small grunts then giving way, remember. I sang at the end, you were funny in the heaviness those roots pulled you back upright. A map we made too for lost.

Must I say then the gift was delicate.

A 1:1 perfume.

oo

We learned vastness from oak, birch and beech
so close we were to colonies;

this is the afterspace

{this is like our little pizza place; this is like our tiny church}

I was amnesiac, hands tattooed onto nubs

He'd walk in and stay, out of my reach
a mezzanine – space as meaningful as the atom

you split you split you split you split

It was better everything was empty

oo

You have to agree with what you are doing

| *this is what I am doing now* | *this is what I am doing now* |

What, I say, will move the legs?

As in the second war,
lamps above us suspended; people
above earth and below

though none of them with bodies –

Not enough space in heaven, they said
to bring leather,

The lamps shone

continuously failing
to accurately tell

our own failings

giving different meaning to the oath
Do No Harm.

oo

Under the portico, [thunder but no storm]

patterned shoulder to shoulder

holy how dizzy how fickle

platforms to dive from

Hereafter not just place but direction.

oo

I tried my best with masts
to spread
but didn't have a flag

only fungus holding my structure in place

I must know, I smoked
we lined up,

<table>
<tr><td>they told us</td><td>red shoes</td></tr>
<tr><td></td><td>hearts</td></tr>
<tr><td>carved into</td><td>pickup trucks</td></tr>
</table>

(their sides) I lie down while old women ride by on bicycles

oo

There was nothing clear about the horizon
barns for boats | no firmament

I would've cut out my own tongue
but no one scene I can remember

It was her red umbrella on the dock, her water taxi
left from a 4 o'clock thunderstorm

        her suitcase covered in spiderwebs
        pulled from the attic of the building
        which tomorrow will be underwater

her hair piece, swimming fins and bad lung

I will not stand in line to enter that house

Half Rest

and wind in the house

fish shaping   and limbs swung

evidence we were plastic   all the damn lights on

through the windows

all that plush plush I had speculation;

there goes the tulip pistil/the orchid bloom

there goes head withering   toward porcelain bowl

half filled with orange

there was wind and it beat on the house
surprised me   she didn't like drafts

so I blocked with my body   when they say minty Morocco tea

and then talk about

how dark her brothers are   she describes it as dark or darker

some people think they are Moroccans   *ooooooh*
they say
the damn lights on

bowls half filled with orange
stamen and the tulip petals splayed like peels

all work all worn the boat traffic stops here

Remembrance Orchestra

His first playing *when the saints go marching in*
on the sax, let's say, badly. [1]

A man learns to keep a house then eats his fist.
I can't say I don't eat meat in your language.

Who knew the *r* should be
back further in my mouth. The cliffs and Dover, just chalk. [2]

Did the life you made shine on you?

Some sent love and some shook hands over deals in passages without knowing the skin over knuckles.

It's palatable to bale hay in round bales between trees
marked by balding.

The din you sleep soundly in a sagging bed. Juice the lemon: it doesn't work for me to count my money like you do.

I like behaving with no natural noise—her name's M and that's it. [3]

---

[1] This is a moment by moment roaming; it will not be civilized.

[2] There is a difference in how one feels towards objects before visiting a place versus how one feels afterwards. I wanted to make these things relevant to my own life, so I felt they were just larger versions of the creekbed where we gathered blue clay in summer. I was shocked that leaving the United Kingdom was as simple as looking back at a wall of white chalk.

[3] On the train, I remembered what Z. said about his lady with no apologies, and it reminded me how dramatic a natural silence can be, especially in crowds.

We pass through dark and curve our tense thighs against it.[4]

Long tunnels where I dream of speaking with glass ornaments of my childhood inside.

Men hover around tables standing straight up and this is sensible.

Ask me late. Ask me righteously.

The train closing the zipper of the distance between us.

And then all the small roads
before this.

I'm a graduate of persistence and traditional courtesies.
I wash my hands. And spit.

Let's have a little skepticism from Ms. Shuler who waved from the old house *don't cross the bridge honey! it's washed away*![5]

Or Ronnie
(peeking under the window, there's the night) Parker knocking.

My little mother opening the door, wide eyed and otherwise plain
Ronnie Parker saying: *Your barn's burnin'.*
So it was.

---

[4] Remember the first time you rode a horse or rode on someone's back. You had to draw a line through your center and squeeze. But this is how you knew where you were.

[5] The flood brought water up above the tires of the '68 green Mustang and mother had to pull over, one kid on her hip, one other held by the hand, and wade through muddy water up to her thighs. Ms. Shuler waved us toward Mitt Dugger's house. The first time I had to walk on my own in spite of the fact that I wanted to be carried.

I can feel the inside of myself farming.[6]

The roots underneath all singed. Z. said: *it's almost like we don't need pharmaceuticals.*

Maybe they huddled. One sow – Big Mama – survived by repeatedly ramming her body into the fence.[7]

The craziest animals we remember.[8]
I am done turning around in the row.

Glass biting locally accepted, small cut mouths.[9]

Clearly we only take our own trains.

Do you need a steam engine when the horse will signify your complete happiness?[10]

She knew I had tried

long as I had been living.

Now a stranger behind I can only see his greasy hair reflected inside the tunnel. Otherwise he is not there.

---

[6] Do you know what I mean when I say tobacco stalks? When did the idea come to make oneself perpetually invisible? We used to hear: don't say that, he'll bite your head off. Or you can ride this bus, as long as you don't breathe too loud. It doesn't identify with home because my voice is not recognizable. There was something purer underneath it anyhow.

[7] What I see are resistances in the body, refusing to speak, refusing to sing. You can take a bus there, get out and walk around them.

[8] We start our friendship by swapping clothes. I've been had. They lured me to the teepee but I am still a Victorian girl being lectured about tatting.

[9] A woman tells me you can have voice with no sound. The vocal cords are an organ of perception. But we get older and close our mouths more.

[10] The girl is more interested in the small folds in fabric and she repeats with her fingertips an action she calls popping, whenever she finds folds. You could think of popping as running through a field of cut tobacco stalks, and if you drag your feet right, you can kick it up and the finger like roots.

How were they able to make these lines so incredibly precise?[11]

Men slurping fruit juice out of plastic bowls. They smell of cigarettes, mold.[12]

All the men taking space, all the minor whimperings.

Years later, my friend sends me a card three inches square, with words in white: *Barn's burnt down. Now I can see the moon.*[13]

What's the big idea about zeitgeist?

I thought about those people and those people got off the train.[14]

---

[11] Do I pay now or later? Do I order at the counter or sit down first? If I sit down, how long will I sit before I give up and go to the counter?

[12] The father rests sullenly in Georgia.

[13] Of course we are always testing the language.

[14] I dreamed we made efforts, nights thought to be castles, one side or another, they came.

Rows of sunflowers, heads turned

toward sun :: surly corn.
                                That looked like
the tassels on tobacco. [15]

Grapevines and rows of grapevines.

Tops of ships, buttresses.

        One secret licking of lips
        that gives hunger a name. [16]

The click of gauche. [17]

The ends of words.   Women
whose names end with the sound of A.

                    Women
                    bald at the crown. [18]

How close I have to stand to smell you.
Not being offered a seat. [19]

Being offered change in coins.

---

[15] Inside the tobacco barn I was finally old enough to strip the stalks. Four or five people side by side at a table, passing a stalk down the line and pulling off the leaves of their grade. You had really made it when you got to strip the tips.

[16] There was that moment when the sea lapped up against the factory. An inner courtyard for picnics between shifts, but who's that lucky.

[17] Rachel Ingram, third grade teacher, slathers on red lipstick then snaps her compact shut, every day, on cue, after lunch.

[18] So I began using the word *body* more and more, just feeling it out, holding it in my hands, if you will, trying it out with a little *fuck you* in it.

[19] Confusing Rosa Parks with Rosa Luxemburg.

Lately he just said *milk* in English.
Playground swings used as hurdles.

Wild lilacs & the vineyard now covered in cheesecloth.[20]
                    Mist over small towns, nestled by castles.

Red shoes and the red left on toes after.

Cabbage moths, bamboo.[21]

                    You can love something
                    & be crushed by it.

Buildings on stilts, red buildings, tiles alternating red and white.

Pines, pines
and white pines. [22]
          Charcoal fires,
          the taste of boulevard.[23]

The esophagus as it leads to the stomach.

Eyelids & the lid of a jar in Tennessee.[24]

The man with his rolled cigarette waiting to get off the train.

---

[20] Early frosts are descended from Abraham, dear.

[21] Overwinters.

[22] Memory like a crease
you can run your hands over. These lines
are incredibly precise.

[23] What is inside is outside. What is out is in. I want to make it clear I don't know in some ways what is happening here.

[24] Some siblings fought over the chore of burning trash and secretly hoped there were plastic milkjugs in the bag.

A friend of the family had a scar on his face from watching a pressurized milkjug explode, but that was years ago.

Curses, the finger. Losing keys in new snow. Resolve.

Spires, windmills, roosters and arrows that swing around them.[25]

The ability to change the state of water. The ability to change states.

Generosity of spirit, especially as it relates to strangers.

Sincere compliments: as in, that might be the nicest thing anyone's ever said to me.[26]

Mothers who shush
their children, especially – it is appropriate.

The habit of
twisting one's hair.[27]

Young girls wearing Wellington boots. Women wearing flat shoes.
Walking toward walls of rain, exclamations of light, unrehearsed.[28]

Elevators that open on both sides.
The short waist.[29]
The man spraying himself with perfume right next to me.[30]

We hunch when we don't know the language.

---

[25] Moments when we couldn't tell both where we were and how fast we were moving.

[26] I used to look at my knees every night and wonder if I would ever see them without bruises.

[27] My mother believed this was the most vain action a young girl could perform in public, and she said so every time I touched my hair.

[28] Book of longing. Supposition.

[29] Estelle's false teeth in a glass on her kitchen windowsill. Hardly a light on in there.

[30] I understood it was crowded.

The man rubbing himself with lotion
right next to me.[31]

The smile of the porter.

Dedicating babies in churches.[32]

Bits of wildness on edges of pristinely designed fields.[33]

Pitchforks long enough for short women.

Brush piles. Fat pigeons trying to mate.[34]

Flock of swallows just before they synchronize in flight.

Continuous view of house between trees.

The burned out car.

The burned out car.[35]

---

[31] Jesus Christ, man.

[32] She wrote a letter to the future and put it in a time capsule.

[33] Often a room in the old house was used as a corncrib if the one in the barn was occupied. Dry corn tossed in on hardwood floors and filled past the windows.

[34] You can make a narrative but take care it is one you will stay loyal to.

[35] How would the tide know where to return?

The people wandering & the people watching

the car.

Those carrying luggage, mainly heavy bags from holidays.
Ones that shuffle or use a cane.
Those reading fashion magazines as they wait.

Those named Pascal. Who does not scold children for being curious. Those shifting eyes. Those carrying food.

Those who think of marriage & those who find the thought of being bound to a house in a village frightful.

Those who forget words at important moments. Those who prefer calling men "mister." The people carrying babies carrying poop in diapers & the people wishing to carry.

Those who snap gum or chew the inside lip.
Those with a childhood home. The smell of bacon. Yellow.

Those that gain the story & those content to be lost.
Those that pillage or ride a bike with no hands. Who should be described as *dapper*.

Those who know they are being led by the nose.
Those that swim the English Channel, frightened by gulls.

Those who believe in some destiny & those who are so full of empathy they take the pain of others. Bruise easy.
Heathen when given the choice. Those able to curl the tongue.

Those eloquent.

Them that talk out of their ass. The ones who allow children to drop keys repeatedly and those who stand against public nuisance. Also those living on top floors.

Eager movers, who find pleasure in longing. Those catalysts, those digging first in spring. Those who make by hand their family's food and clothing.

Those who rob & those who put back.
Those who keep & those who caution those that keep.

The dawn, & the making of dawn.
And dusk. What is lost is dusk.[36]

[36] I will never come this way again.

Notes

p31: line in italics is taken from choreographer and dancer Deborah Hay.

The second 'Tuning' section is made partially from excerpts of the letters of Katherine Rosson and of Estelle Dickey, written to the author.

p66: line in italics is from Michael Palmer.

'Remembrance Orchestra' first appeared in a chapbook called *Apparatus for Manufacturing Sunset* from dancing girl press.

Lightning Source UK Ltd.
Milton Keynes UK
UKHW011950140819
347976UK00001B/123/P

9 781848 616592